Sugar Inspirations

Roses in Sugar

CHRIS JEFFCOATE & JACKIE KUFLIK

MEREHURST

Dedication

Chris and Jackie would like to thank Doris and Gladys, without whom this book would not have been written. This book is dedicated to our children, with our love.

First published 1997 by Merehurst Limited
Ferry House, 51–57 Lacy Road, Putney,
London SW15 1PR

Copyright © Merehurst Limited 1997
ISBN 1-85391-655-2

A catalogue record for this book is available from the British Library.

Editor: Helen Southall
Design: Anita Ruddell
Photography by James Duncan and Clive Streeter

Colour separation by Bright Arts, Hong Kong
Printed in Hong Kong by Wing King Tong

Acknowledgements

The authors would like to thank the following suppliers:

Cake Art Ltd.
Venture Way,
Crown Estate,
Priorswood,
Taunton,
Devon TA2 8DE
Tel: 01823 321532

J. F. Renshaw Ltd.
Crown Street,
Liverpool L8 7RF
Tel: 0151 706 8200

Sugar Celebrations
176A Manchester Road,
Swindon,
Wilts. SN1 1TU
Tel: 01793 513549

The publishers would also like to thank the following:

Guy, Paul and Co. Ltd.
Unit B4,
Foundry Way,
Little End Road,
Eaton Socon,
Cambs. PE19 3JH
Tel: 01480 472545

Squires Kitchen
Squires House,
3 Waverley Lane,
Farnham,
Surrey GU9 8BB
Tel: 01252 711749

Anniversary House (Cake Decorations) Ltd.
Unit 5, Elliott Road,
Roundways,
Bournemouth,
Hants. BH11 8JJ
Tel: 01202 590222

Contents

Introduction

The natural beauty of the rose, combined with its symbolic and historic associations, make it an ever-popular sugarcraft subject.

Roses modelled in sugar can be as varied as the real flowers themselves. The wonderful colour possibilities, and the huge range of varieties, make them infinitely adaptable for use in both large and small sprays, on their own or mixed with other flowers and foliage, and on celebration cakes of all sorts. There are so many varieties to choose from that we had some difficulty deciding which roses to feature in this book.

The simplest rose is the 'wild' rose, *Rosa canina* (the English briar). The modern hybrid tea rose, which originally smelled faintly of tea, and the old-fashioned rose, sometimes known as the musk or moss rose, are both popular varieties. The old-fashioned rose tends to be a floribunda, meaning that it produces many flowers on one stem, whereas the hybrid tea is usually a single-stemmed rose. As gardens get smaller, so more miniature varieties are being developed for growing in pots, indoors and out.

According to research, roses have existed on Earth for some 35 million years – longer than man! Many stories and traditions concerning the rose have made it an emblem of love and secrecy; Cupid carries roses as well as a bow and arrow. The Greek island of Rhodes is named after the rose, and the original rosary was a string of beads made with tightly packed rose petals that gave off a sweet fragrance.

Over the centuries, the rose has been used in decorations of all sorts: wood carvings of roses can often be found in churches and country houses; the rose features frequently in heraldry; today the rose is a central source for designs in jewellery, fabrics, glass and ornamentation.

It is hardly surprising, therefore, that the rose should be so popular in sugarcraft. We hope that the roses we have chosen to feature in this book will inspire you to use sugar roses in new and exciting ways, perhaps basing your designs on the fascinating history of this beautiful flower.

Equipment

We have used our 'basic kit' for most of the roses featured in this book, but particular tools and cutters have been noted under the relevant instructions. Templates are also provided on pages 45–48.

Non-stick board and rolling pin
A board that has grooves on the reverse side is useful for creating the central veins of leaves, allowing easy insertion of wires.

Non-stick pad
This is used to support petals as you work them with modelling tools. You can use the palm of your hand, but this can be tiring and the paste can become sticky.

Paintbrushes
Round brushes, from size 00000 upwards, are useful for painting fine lines. A flat 1cm (½ inch) dusting brush gives broad, even coverage of powder colour, whilst a fan brush gives a fine application of dust to very delicate petals.

Dowel rod and cocktail sticks (toothpicks)
When new, these wooden tools can stick, so rub them well with a small amount of white vegetable fat (shortening) before use.

Craft knife or scalpel
Useful for neatening rough edges of petals, or nicking the petals to give a ragged effect.

Scissors
Two pairs are required: a fine pair for cutting paste and a heavy-duty

pair (or wire cutters) for cutting wires.

Flexible palette knife
Useful for lifting petals from the non-stick board to the pad or the palm of your hand.

Tweezers
A pointed pair of long-nose tweezers is useful for putting hooks in wires and for teasing petals into position.

Wires
White and green wires, ranging from 30-gauge, for individually wired petals, to 24-gauge for the centres of roses, are required. Stub wires are needed for very heavy roses.

Modelling tools
A variety of sizes of ball tool is available. The smaller the ball, the sharper the curve of the petal will be. Dogbone tools give a different curve to petals.

Stamens
Commercially available stamens can be used, or you can make your own with cotton thread (see page 36).

Florists' tape
Used to cover the wires, florists' tape is usually cut lengthways in half for easier handling and a finer finish. It can also be used to add bulk to stems.

Colours
We have used paste, liquid and powder colours (petal dusts/blossom tints), depending upon the paste and the finish required (see individual instructions).

Cutters and veiners
We recommend a good set of rose petal cutters in a wide range of sizes (see templates on page 48). Commercially made cutters are available for different types of roses and we have identified these where necessary. You will also need leaf and calyx cutters in a range of sizes. Leaf veiners are also available in wide variety. We have used double-sided veiners that allow us to display the backs as well as the fronts of the leaves.

Glue
We have used the term 'glue' throughout this book. You can use fresh egg white (although we do not recommend this for flowers that are to be used on a cake due to the slight risk of salmonella being present) or you can use one of the following:

1 Pure rose water (25ml/ 5 teaspoons) with a sprinkling of gum tragacanth or gum arabic. Place in a small jar and shake well to mix. Leave to mature for 2 hours before using.

2 Pure rose water (25ml/ 5 teaspoons) with a large pea of flower paste dropped in. The paste will soften and eventually dissolve.

3 Pure rose water (25ml/ 5 teaspoons) with 2–3g (about ½ teaspoon) of pure albumen. Place in a small jar and shake well to mix. Leave to mature for about 2 hours before using.

4 Plain cooled boiled water or plain rose water.

Piped Roses

Piped royal icing roses make a pretty addition to any cake, large or small,
and are totally edible.

For piping roses, the royal icing should be quite stiff (see recipe on page 44). If available, add a few drops of acetic acid to the icing; this will make the icing stronger and the petals 'break away' easily from each other as they are piped. Most piped flowers are made on a flower nail, with small squares of grease-proof or waxed paper stuck to the nail with a little royal icing. Alternatively, you can use a specially designed rose nail or 'cone' that has a non-stick surface and needs no paper. When the rose is dry it can be gently pushed off the nail.

A variety of petal piping tubes (tips) is available for both left- and right-handed use. The number of the tube depicts the size of the finished rose. For the roses illustrated, we have used a no. 57 tube, and the steps on pages 7–8 show both the right- and left-handed methods of piping.

Finishing piped roses

Piped roses can be finished off by adding a calyx to each one; rose leaves can be piped at the same time. When each piped rose has set, remove it carefully from the piping cone and fill the back with royal icing piped with a no. 1 tube. Leave to dry, then pipe on a calyx with a no. 1 tube and green royal icing. Leave to dry.

Rose leaves can be piped using green royal icing and either a leaf tube or a greaseproof paper piping bag with a small 'V' cut in the pointed end. Use piped roses individually, or arrange them in small groups with leaves, securing with royal icing.

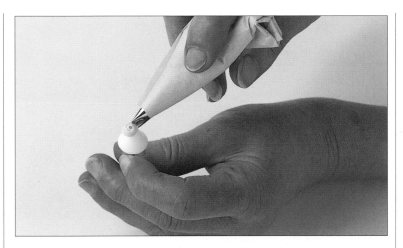

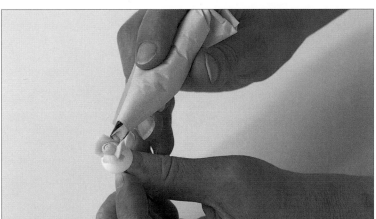

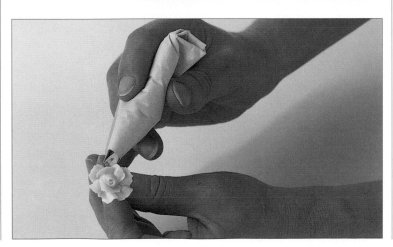

Right-handed piping

1 Hold the piping bag so that the tube (tip) is in a vertical position, with the pointed end at the top, over the centre of the rose cone. Pipe a bud by squeezing the icing out to stick to the cone, and then turning the nail 360° in an anti-clockwise direction, finishing with a downwards action to break the icing off.

2 Pipe the first row of three petals, this time positioning the narrow point of the tube out slightly, and using an upwards and then a downwards motion to create each petal, turning the nail at the same time (anti-clock-wise).

3 Add the final row of five petals, using the same method as before. Leave to dry on the cone, then remove and finish as described on page 6.

Left-handed piping

1 Hold the piping bag so that the tube (tip) is in a vertical position, with the pointed end at the top, over the centre of the rose cone. Pipe a bud by squeezing the icing out to stick to the cone, and then turning the nail 360° in a clockwise direction, and finishing with a downwards action to break the icing off.

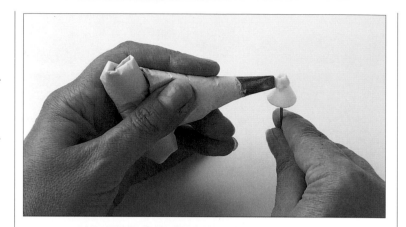

2 Pipe the first row of three petals, this time positioning the narrow point of the tube out slightly, and using an upwards and then a downwards motion to create each petal, turning the nail at the same time (clockwise).

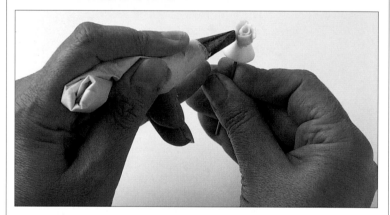

3 Add the final row of five petals, using the same method as before. Leave to dry on the cone, then remove and finish as described on page 6.

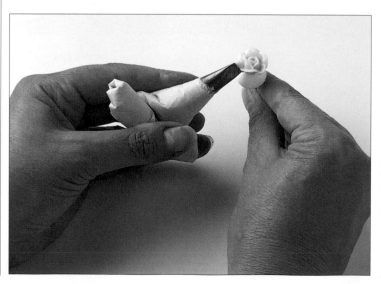

Rosebud Cake

The two-tone rosebuds on this pretty cake are piped using two colours of icing in the same bag.

Materials

20cm (8 inch) round cake
25cm (10 inch) round cake drum
Apricot glaze
1kg (2lb) marzipan (almond paste)
1kg (2lb) royal icing
Green and peach food colourings
Ribbon to trim cake drum

Equipment

Stainless-steel icing ruler
Stainless-steel side scraper
Plastic side scraper with double groove pattern
Paper piping bags
Nos. 1, 2, 3 and 44 piping tubes (tips)
No. 57 petal and small leaf piping tubes (tips)

Preparation

1 Place the cake centrally on the cake drum. Brush the cake with boiled apricot glaze, and coat the top and sides with marzipan. Leave to set for 24 hours.

2 Apply white royal icing in three coats, leaving to dry between applications. The final side coating should be scraped clean using the patterned side scraper, taking great care with the lift off. Coat the board with royal icing. Leave to dry completely.

Decoration

3 Pipe an arrangement of lines on the top of the cake with green royal icing and a no. 1 tube. Fill a piping bag fitted with a petal tube with peach and white royal icing, placing the peach icing on the same side of the bag as the fine point of the tube, and the white icing on the opposite side.

4 To pipe the rosebuds, position the fat end of the tube on the cake surface. Holding the bag at an angle of 45° to the cake, squeeze the icing out of the bag without moving the tube at all, until a round bud is formed. Stop squeezing and lift the tube off. Continue in this way until a full spray of rosebuds is produced.

5 Pipe a small green calyx with a no. 1 tube on to the base of each bud. Pipe tiny thorns along the stems. Pipe

leaves with a small leaf tube, again held at an angle of 45°. Squeeze and lift repeatedly, causing a serrated edge to the leaf, gradually releasing the pressure until a point is formed at the tip of the leaf.

6 Repeat the piping of the stems, rosebuds, calyxes, thorns and leaves around the side of the cake, between the two raised borders.

7 For the scroll decoration on the top of the cake, pipe a repeated 'C' scroll in white royal icing with a no. 44 tube around the top edge of the cake. Overpipe the scrolls with a no. 3, then a no. 2 tube in white royal icing, and finish with a no. 1 tube and peach icing. Pipe an inscription if required.

8 Pipe a base shell border with white royal icing and a no. 44 tube. Overpipe loops with a no. 3, and then a no. 2 tube in white royal icing, and finish with a no. 1 tube and peach royal icing. Trim the cake drum with ribbon.

Ruby Wedding Cake

We have made this design into a cake celebrating a ruby wedding anniversary, but with templates for all numerals on page 45, you can change the numbers and colours to suit any occasion.

Materials

1kg (2lb) cream royal icing made with pure albumen
Pink petal dust (blossom tint)
Cream, pink, green and brown food colourings
15cm (6 inch) round cake
20cm (8 inch) round cake drum
Apricot glaze
500g (1lb) marzipan (almond paste)
Glycerine
Ribbon to trim cake drum

Equipment

Paper piping bags
Nos. 0, 1, 2, 3 and 57 piping tubes (tips)
Desk lamp
Rose piping nail
Stainless-steel icing ruler
Stainless-steel side scraper
Piece of soft sponge

Preparation

1 Make runout sugar numerals using the templates on page 45. Leave to dry under a desk lamp. Dust with pink. Make 42 piped roses (see pages 6–8), using royal icing coloured with pink and a touch of brown. Leave to dry.

2 Place the cake centrally on the cake drum. Brush the cake with boiled apricot glaze, and coat the top and then the sides with marzipan. Leave to set for 24 hours.

3 Beat the remaining royal icing carefully, mixing in 3 teaspoons glycerine, to make a softer cutting coat. Apply the royal icing, in 2–3 coats, leaving to dry between applications. Coat the board around the cake with royal icing.

Decoration

4 Using paper templates (page 48), pipe the centre linework using nos. 3, 2 and 1 tubes. Pipe lines from the centre, dividing the cake into quarters. Pipe 3-2-1 lines from the dividing lines to the cake edge. Next, pipe side panels, using a paper template, if needed.

5 Decorate the board with 3-2-1 piping to match the side panel design. Using a no. 0 tube, pipe cornelli work on the centre top and bottom sides of the cake. Pipe bulbs around the base of the cake, and pipe green scrolls as shown in the picture opposite.

6 Finally, attach the roses and numerals with a little royal icing, supporting the numerals if necessary with a piece of soft sponge until set. Trim the cake drum with a length of ribbon.

Marzipan Roses

Flowers that are completely edible are a delight to one and all, and they are quick and enjoyable to make.

Marzipan (almond paste) is easily modelled. It remains soft and pliable for quite a time and takes colour very well. Although you can make a special marzipan for modelling (see page 44), commercially available marzipan can be readily used.

Keep the marzipan wrapped in polythene bags when you are not using it. If you overknead marzipan it can become oily (this is the almond oil being worked out of the paste). If this happens, mix in a few drops of orange flower water or rose water, leave to rest in a polythene bag and wash your hands in cool water. If the marzipan is sticky, wipe your fingers with a damp cloth. (It is a good idea to keep a damp cloth beside you at all times when modelling with marzipan.) Generally, marzipan will stick to itself if fresh. However, if you have left pieces to dry, then glue them together with a little melted chocolate (white is ideal). Don't use royal icing as this will crack away from the marzipan as it dries.

Rose

1 Model a pear-shaped piece of marzipan and flat-

ten one side with the side of your hand. Fold the tip of the flattened paste inwards, and then roll the paste up along the flattened edge. Shape a bud and leave to stand on the excess paste.

2 Place two small balls of marzipan inside a polythene bag. Flatten one side of each ball, then thin the flattened side and leave a thicker pad of marzipan on the other side. Work on the two petals at the same time to keep them the same size.

3 Wrap the two petals around the bud, overlapping the edges.

4 Flatten three more slightly larger petals in the same way, and wrap around the first layer of petals, overlapping as before.

5 Whilst the paste is still pliable, shape the petals with your fingertips, curling the

edges back to give a more realistic appearance.

6 ⟩ Roll the back of the flower between your forefingers to make a rose shape.

7 ⟩ Finally, cut the excess paste away from the base

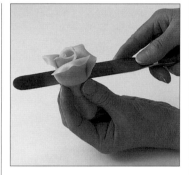

of the finished rose with a palette knife. Add calyxes cut from green marzipan if required.

Leaves

8 ⟩ Roll out green marzipan on a non-stick board, and cut out leaves using a rose leaf cutter.

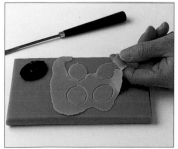

9 ⟩ Lift the leaves away from the board with a fine palette knife and vein in double-sided veiners. Pinch the back of the central vein at the base to enhance the shaping of the leaf.

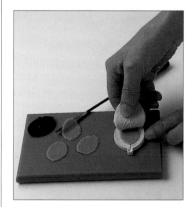

Plaque

10 ⟩ Coat a cake board with white marzipan. Polish well with the flat of your hand or a smoother, and emboss the edge with a shell modelling tool. Make roses, buds and leaves as shown above, and arrange on the coated board, securing with cooled, boiled water. Alternatively, arrange directly on a cake (see page 16).

Marzipan Birthday Cake

Using marzipan as a finished surface and decorative medium can give a less sweet taste than a traditionally iced cake. The cake base can be fruit cake (heavy or light), genoese sponge or victoria sandwich.

Materials

20cm (8 inch) round cake
25cm (10 inch) round cake drum
Apricot glaze
1.5kg (3lb) white marzipan
(almond paste)
Pink and green food colourings
Small amount of royal icing

Equipment

Icing smoothers
Straight crimper
Polythene bag
Calyx cutter
Rose leaf cutters
Fine palette knife
Rose leaf veiners
Paper piping bag
No. 1 piping tube (tip)

Preparation

1 Place the cake in the centre of the cake drum, and coat with boiled apricot glaze. Knead 1kg (2lb) of the marzipan well, and roll it out to a thickness of 2.5mm (⅛ inch). Lift on to the cake, using the rolling pin as a support. Smooth well over the top and sides of the cake, gently easing the bottom edge in neatly at the base. Polish with icing smoothers. Trim the excess away with a sharp knife and repolish the cake.

2 Colour some marzipan pink and roll it out to a long sausage to fit the circumference of the cake. Glue to the bottom edge of the cake with a little boiled water. Trim away the surplus and smooth the join with your fingertips.

3 Crimp the sausage using a straight crimper, keeping the jaws of the crimper moistened with a clean damp cloth to prevent it sticking to the marzipan.

Flowers

4 Following the instructions on pages 14–15, make one fully open marzipan rose, one half open rose and five rosebuds. Make about 10 marzipan rose leaves. Arrange decoratively on the top of the cake, and secure with cooled, boiled water. Position one leaf over the crimped base border.

5 Make a small marzipan plaque using either a sharp knife or a cutter, and pipe on it the inscription with royal icing and a no. 1 tube (see alphabet templates on page 46). Place in position on the cake when the piping has set.

16

Cutter Rose

This rose is made from flower paste, the size of the rose
being determined by the size of the cutters used.

Materials

24-gauge wires
Glue, page 5
Flower paste, page 44
Pink petal dust (blossom tint)
Cream and green food colourings
Florists' tape
Stub wires, optional

Equipment

Tweezers
Rose petal cutters or templates,
page 48
Dogbone tool
Cocktail stick (toothpick)
Calyx cutter

Rose

1 Bend a hook in one end of a 24-gauge wire with

tweezers, and moisten with glue. Place a piece of flower paste on the hooked end, and shape into a cone that will be the centre of the rose. The cone should fit inside the smaller chosen petal cutter. Leave to dry.

2 Roll out some flower paste, and cut out one petal with a small cutter. Soften the edges with a dogbone tool, and paint the surface of the petal with glue. Wrap the petal tightly around the cone so that the cone cannot be seen down through the top of the rolled petal. Leave to dry.

3 Cut out a second petal, soften the edges, and glue the bottom half. Wrap this

around the first petal, opening the top edge slightly.

4 Cut two more petals and repeat the process above, this time adding the two petals at the same time and overlapping the edges. Cut three more petals and repeat the process above, this time adding all three petals at the same time. Open up the top edges of the petals and curl them back slightly with your fingertips.

5 The rose will now have grown in size. Select a rose petal cutter one size larger than the one you started with and cut four or five petals. Soften the edges with a dogbone tool and cup the centre, then

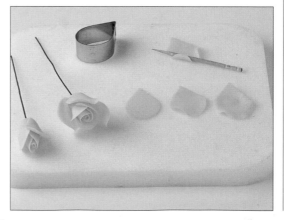

turn the petal over and soften the edges again with a dogbone tool. Use a cocktail stick to curl back the edges of each petal from the sides of the top edge. Leave to become leathery (about 5 minutes) before brushing glue on the bottom third of each petal, and adding them to the flower.

6 Shape the petals further with your fingertips. You can choose at this stage to add another layer or to stop. If you decide to stop, check around the whole flower to ensure that joins are neat and that the petals have a good shape.

7 When firm, dust the roses with powder colour, using a flat brush and pink petal dust. Steam the flowers lightly, by passing them quickly through the steam from a boiling kettle, to set the colour.

Calyx

8 Roll out some green and cream flower paste very thinly. Lay the cream on top of the green and cut out a calyx. To obtain the correct size, one finger (sepal) of the calyx cutter should be slightly shorter than the small petal cutter used. Cut small snips down the side of each sepal, then soften all the

19

edges with a dogbone tool, working on the green side. Turn the calyx over and cup the centre. Brush the centre with glue and push the calyx up the wire behind the rose. Gently press on to the back of the flower. Roll a small pea of green paste, glue it and push it up the wire to the back of the calyx. Smooth neatly into position.

Spray

9 Tape the wires with half-width florists' tape, two or three times, to make the stems more realistic in thickness. If the roses are very large, and therefore heavy, add a stub wire to the original 24-gauge wire to give extra strength. Make leaves (see pages 21–22) and rosebuds (which are made like the flower but without the open and curled petals) and wire into a natural arrangement.

Rose Leaves

The basic technique for rose leaves, once mastered, can be applied to nearly any leaf.

Materials

Flower paste, page 44
Green food colouring
26 and 28-gauge green wires
Glue, page 5
Apple green, moss and red or burgundy petal dusts (blossom tints)
Confectioners' varnish, optional
Florists' tape

Equipment

Rose leaf cutters
Foam pad
Dogbone tool
Double-sided leaf veiners

Leaf

1 Roll out some green flower paste, angling the rolling pin slightly to create a wedge of thicker paste.

Alternatively, use a grooved rolling pin or board. Cut out a leaf, positioning the cutter so that the ridge of thicker paste is at the base of the leaf.

2 Place the leaf on the palm of your hand or a pad of hard foam and soften the edge with the back of a dogbone tool.

3 Dip a 26 or 28-gauge wire (depending on the size of the leaf) into glue, and then carefully push it into the ridge of paste in the leaf.

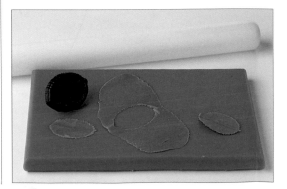

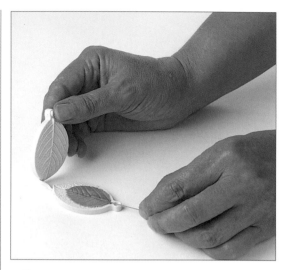

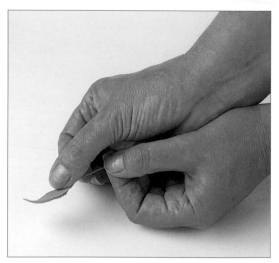

4 Smooth the join and ensure that the wire is firmly embedded into the paste.

5 Vein the leaf in a double-sided leaf veiner. Remove the leaf and pinch the back of the large centre vein at the base with your thumb and forefinger to give greater definition to the front of the centre vein.

Colouring

6 Colour the leaf with petal dusts. Apply a little apple green to one side of the leaf and moss to the other, blending through the middle. Add a touch of red or burgundy to the edges, as required, and steam to give a natural gloss (see page 19). Once the leaf is dry, if you wish to have a greater shine on the leaf, paint the top surface with confectioners' varnish.

Spray

7 Cut some florists' tape lengthways in half and use to tape the leaves together in natural sprays of three or five leaves. Alternatively, leaves can be used individually in arrangements, if required.

Gâteau Vert

Large gingko leaves make a good background for the delicately coloured roses in the arrangements on this unusually shaped cake.

Materials

18cm (7 inch) square cake
25cm (10 inch) square cake board
Apricot glaze
1kg (2lb) marzipan (almond paste)
1kg (2lb) sugarpaste (rolled fondant)
Green food colouring
Silver snowflake lustre dust
Ribbon to trim cake board
Small amount of flower paste
4 royal icing doves, optional

Equipment

Icing smoothers
Tape measure
Texture mat
Pointed dowel
Flower pick

Flowers

11 cream cutter roses (various sizes), page 18
15 white blossom buds
12–15 white blossoms (pulled method)
12 gingko leaves, page 24

Preparation

1 Cut away one corner of the square cake on a line running between the centres of two adjacent sides. Position the cake on the square board so that the two uncut sides are 2.5cm (1 inch) from the edges of the board.

2 Brush the cake with apricot glaze. Roll out the marzipan and use to cover both the top and sides of the cake in one piece. Trim with a sharp knife and polish to a smooth finish. Leave to dry.

3 Colour all but 125g (4oz) of the sugarpaste with green colouring and roll out so that the paste will cover the top and sides of the cake, and the board, all in one piece. Smooth well with the smoothers, ensuring a neat fit all round. Trim off the excess paste from the board edges.

Sugar ribbon

4 Measure the circumference of the cake. Roll out the white sugarpaste and texture it on a texture mat. Cut to a strip long enough to fit round the cake and 2.5cm (1 inch) wide. Dust with silver snowflake lustre dust. Glue to the cake with a little cooled, boiled water, making the join at the back neat. Trim the cake board with ribbon.

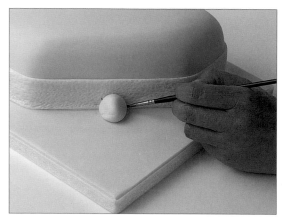

Flowers

⟨5⟩ Mark the positioning of the flower pick with a pointed dowel, and then push the pick into the cake, leaving a small amount of the plastic above the surface of the cake. Leave the cake to dry.

⟨6⟩ Wire together approximately half of all the flowers into a spray for the top of the cake and position in the flower pick.

⟨7⟩ Shape a small cone of flower paste, moisten the back with a little cooled, boiled water, and position it at the front of the cake. Leave to set for approximately 15 minutes.

⟨8⟩ Arrange the remaining flowers and leaves by pushing them carefully into the cone of flower paste only. **Do not push the flowers into the sugarpaste on the cake**. If the wires are too long, trim to a suitable length.

Finishing

⟨9⟩ If liked, attach two pairs of royal icing doves to the top of the cake and the board, using a little royal icing.

Gingko leaves

Gingko leaves are made in much the same way as rose leaves (see page 21), using gingko leaf cutters and veiners. Dust with apple green, adding brown around the edges.

Five-Petal Cutter Rose

This rose uses a very quick method, allowing you to make and attach five petals at the same time. However, this is not the easiest method. Some dexterous practice with your fingers will be necessary before you get it right!

Materials

24-gauge green wires
Glue, page 5
Flower paste, page 44

Equipment

Tweezers
5-petal blossom cutter
Dogbone tool
Calyx cutter

Flower

1 Bend a hook in one end of a 24-gauge wire with tweezers, and dip in glue. Form a piece of flower paste into a pointed teardrop shape. To check the size, hold the teardrop against the blossom cutter; the teardrop should just fit inside one petal. Leave to dry.

2 Roll out some paste thinly and cut out one set of petals with the cutter. Soften the edges and cup the centre of each petal with a dogbone tool. Paint a little glue in the centre area and over the entire surface of one petal. Push the wire through the centre and wrap the glued petal around the cone. Glue the bottom half of one of the petals opposite the first and wrap this lightly around the first. Finally, half glue the other three petals and wrap them evenly and loosely around to create the first layer of petals.

3 Cut another set of petals, half glue these and push the wire through the centre. Wrap one petal around the first layer, then one on the opposite

side, and finally the other three petals. Shape and curl back the edges of the petals to make the flower more open. Leave to dry.

Calyx

4 Cut a calyx from green paste, soften the edges with the dogbone tool, and glue to the back of the flower. Add a small pea of green paste and smooth into place.

Hogarth Rose Spray

This elegant spray consists of five-petal cutter roses and foliage arranged in a Hogarth curve. For advice on colouring roses, see pages 40–43.

Materials

Green florists' tape
3mm (⅛ inch) double-faced satin ribbon (sand dune)

Flowers

5 medium rose leaves, page 21
20 small rose leaves
10 tiny rose leaves
15 tiny white rosebuds
10 small yellow roses
11 tiny white roses
5 medium pink/peach roses
1 large tangerine rose, page 18

Leaves

1 Wire together the small and tiny leaves into mixed sets of five. The medium leaves are used individually.

Large return

2 Arrange nine tiny white rosebuds in a natural cluster, making sure one bud is longer than the rest. Curl the wires slightly as you enter them into the spray, and tape together using half-width tape. Add a set of five leaves.

3 Start adding small ribbon loops and small roses, adding more leaf clusters as necessary. As the return progresses, you will need to offer larger roses and leaves. In all, the large return contains eleven tiny rosebuds, three tiny roses, five small roses and one medium rose. To help achieve a natural look we have added small stems of covered wire made to look like rose thorns (see page 28).

tape securely, using full-width tape. Tape in some long, trailing ribbons. Cut away excess wires at the base of the stem and cover the base of the stem with tape to give a neat finish.

9 Look at the finished spray and arrange into a Hogarth curve by curling the top return in one direction (to the right) and the base return in the opposite direction (to the left). Bend the leaf and thorn stems to give a natural look.

Thorn stems

Cover a piece of 28-gauge wire with tape. Make thorns by rolling pieces of half-width tape into a point and taping to the covered wire.

Small return

4 Make a smaller return in a similar way, using two tiny rosebuds, three tiny roses, two small roses and one medium rose.

Centre

5 To make the centre of the spray, form a cluster of five ribbon loops, and tape them together. Offer the large rose to the middle of the ribbon cluster, and place three medium roses around the edge.

6 Make two very small returns, making both slightly different to give a more natural appearance. For one, use one tiny rosebud, three tiny roses and one small rose. For the other, use one tiny rosebud, two tiny roses and two small roses.

7 Add the two very small returns to the central cluster and tape together firmly,

bending the wires to meet the central stem.

Finishing

8 Place the three parts of the spray together and

Tablecloth Cake

A variety of interesting effects can be created with this technique.
The base coat of sugarpaste can be thinner than usual as an extra layer of sugarpaste
(the 'tablecloth') is applied.

Materials

20cm (8 inch) round cake
.25cm (10 inch) round cake drum
Apricot glaze
1kg (2lb) marzipan (almond paste)
1kg (2lb) sugarpaste (rolled fondant)
Pink food colouring
125g (4oz) flower paste
Small amount of royal icing
3mm (⅛ inch) satin ribbon
Ribbon to trim cake drum

Equipment

Icing smoothers
Cocktail sticks (toothpicks)
Paper piping bags
Nos. 1 and 2 piping tubes (tips)
Nos. 1 and 2 paintbrushes

Decorations

3 unwired rosebuds (cutter method, page 18)
Small unwired rose leaves, page 21
3 sets of ribbon loops

Preparation

1 Position the cake centrally on the drum, and brush with apricot glaze. Roll out the marzipan to cover both the top and sides of the cake in one piece. Fit the marzipan on to the cake, ensuring a neat, smooth finish. Trim with a sharp knife and polish with smoothers. Leave to dry.

2 Roll out pink sugarpaste so that there is enough to coat the cake and drum at the same time. Brush the marzipan with a little cooled, boiled water and lift the sugarpaste into position, smoothing well with your hands or smoothers.

'Tablecloth'

3 Measure the diameter of the cake. Add 7.5cm (3 inches) to this measurement and make a paper template, cutting either a plain circle or one with a patterned edge (see page 47). Mix together a paste made up of 25% flower paste and 75% sugarpaste, and knead well.

4 Roll out the paste as thinly as possible on a non-stick board. Hold the template lightly on the surface and cut round the template with a sharp knife or scalpel. Remove the template and polish the surface of the paste with the flat of your hand or an icing smoother.

5 Use a rolling pin to lift the paste and lower it into position on the top of the cake. Do **not** moisten the surface of

30

the cake. Remove the rolling pin and adjust the 'cloth' so that it drapes evenly over the cake. Create even folds around the edge of the 'cloth' with your fingers (see Note below).

6 Lift the 'cloth' higher in six evenly spaced places around the cake, and hold in position with cocktail sticks pushed into the cake. Leave the cocktail sticks in position until the 'cloth' has had time to dry and set completely (about 1 hour).

Note

It is important to work quickly when positioning and shaping the 'cloth' (steps 5 and 6), otherwise the sugarpaste might start to dry, causing cracks as you lift it.

Finishing

7 Remove the cocktail sticks and conceal the holes with the rosebuds, rose leaves and ribbon loops, fixing them in position with a little royal icing.

8 Trace the pattern (page 46) on to the top of the cake, and brush embroider the flowers and leaves with royal icing coloured as required. Use a no. 2

piping tube and brush for the roses, and a no. 1 tube and brush for the leaves. Leave to dry.

9 Finally, pipe small shells or bulbs around the base of the cake, fixing a 3mm (⅛ inch) ribbon in position as you pipe. Pipe fine embroidery or a dropped loop pattern on the edge of the 'cloth'. Complete the piping on top of the cake. Trim the cake drum with ribbon.

Old-Fashioned Rose

Ideally, this rose is best made when a real one is available to copy.

Materials

33-gauge white wires
Flower paste, page 44
Christmas red and green paste food colourings
Glue, page 5
Fine yellow and white cotton
White and green florists' tape
Old gold liquid food colouring
Stub wires
Pink, skintone and white petal dusts (blossom tints)
Rose leaves, page 21

Equipment

Tweezers
Rose petal cutters or templates, page 48
Dogbone tool
Fine paintbrush
Cocktail stick (toothpick)
Calyx cutter

Rose centre

1 Cut some 33-gauge white wires into short lengths, and bend a small hook in one end of each with tweezers.

2 Colour some flower paste with a tiny amount of Christmas red colouring to produce a very, very pale pink. Roll and cut out a petal using the smallest cutter you can find, and soften the edges with a dogbone tool. Moisten the surface of the petal with glue and wrap it around the hooked wire.

3 Cut another three tiny petals, soften the edges, and then wrap them around the first petal, one at a time, pinching all the petals together at the bottom and allowing the top edges to splay out. For each rose, make six of these petal groups.

4 Wind some fine yellow and white cotton together around three of your fingers approximately 30 times. Remove the loop of cotton, twist into a figure of eight, and then twist on a 33-gauge white wire. Tape the loop on to the wire so that the cotton stands up. Trim the top of the loops away, leaving approximately 1cm (½ inch). Using a fine paintbrush, paint the tips of the cotton with old gold liquid colouring. Leave to dry.

5 Place the six groups of petals around the stamens and tape together. They will fit

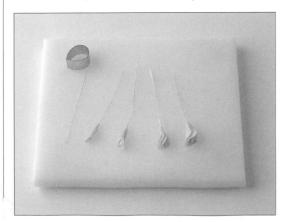

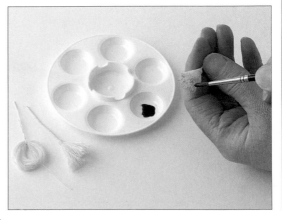

together better if the petals are not completely hard. Tape this assembly to a stub wire, and then cover the wire with green tape.

Petals

 6 Cut three large petals, soften the edges well with a dogbone tool, and paint glue on the bottom half of each. Wrap around the rose centre, overlapping the petals as you go and forming a neat, round shape.

7 Cut out more large petals and soften the edges. The petals should be well tooled and the top edges curled back well with a cocktail stick. Leave to firm up for at least 10 minutes before adding them to the rose. Start by adding three petals in one layer, then four and then five for the final layer, allowing each layer to set well before adding the next.

8 Hang the rose upside-down until the glue has set, and then turn it the right way up to allow the petals to drop back slightly. (Watch this carefully! If the petals drop too far, turn the rose upside-down again to allow the glue to set firmer.)

9 When the rose is completely dry, colour the edges of the petals with a very light dusting of the palest pink petal dust (pink, skintone and white mixed). Steam quickly (see page 19) and add a calyx.

Arrangement

10 Make as many roses as required and wire them up with plenty of leaves. Arrange in a vase, bending the stems into natural curves.

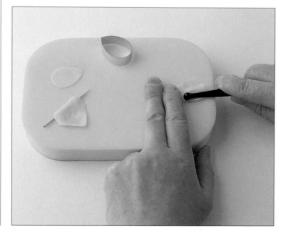 

Briar Rose

This dainty little rose can add lightness to a small cake where hybrid tea roses would look heavy and out of place.

Materials

Yellow and white cotton thread
30-gauge white wires
Flower paste, page 44
Glue, page 5
Pale green and pink petal dusts
Iso-propyl alcohol
Old gold liquid food colouring
24-gauge green wires
Green and white florists' tape
Green paste food colouring
Rose leaves, page 21

Equipment

Briar rose or heart-shaped
petal cutter
Dogbone tool
Flat dusting brush
Calyx cutters
Tiny plain rose petal cutter or
template, page 48

Rose centre

1. Wrap some fine yellow and white cotton around two fingers approximately 30 times. Remove from your fingers, twist into a figure of eight, and then secure on to a 30-gauge white wire. Trim the cotton to about 5mm (¼ inch) long, and comb into a circle with the tip of a scalpel.

2. Make a small pill of white flower paste, flatten and glue into the centre of the stamens. Push the end of a paintbrush into the centre of the paste to make a small dent. Paint the paste with a little green dust mixed with iso-propyl alcohol to give a shaded finish. Colour the tips of the stamens and the centre dent with old gold liquid colouring. Tape the assembly with ¼-width white tape.

Petals

3. Roll out some white flower paste, leaving a slightly thicker ridge of paste. Cut out five petals so that the tops are thin and the pointed ends are slightly thickened. Dip 30-gauge white wires in glue, and insert into the thickened tips of the petals. Soften the edges of the petals with a dogbone tool, allowing the petal edges to curve naturally. Leave to dry.

4. Dust the edges of the petals with a little pink dust to give just a blush of colour. Use a flat brush, stroking

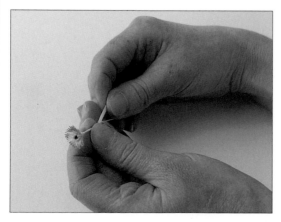

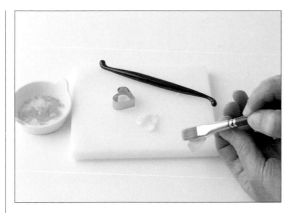

the colour across the edge of the petal towards the centre.

Assembly

5 Tape the flower centre on to a 24-gauge green wire with green tape.

6 Add the first four petals, overlapping the edges. Add the last petal, which lays over the top of the two either side of it. Pull the wires of the petals downwards to obtain a

snug fit, and then tape securely into position.

7 Cut a calyx from green paste, soften the edges and cup the centres of the sepals, and then glue into position. Leave to dry.

Buds

8 Using a tiny plain rose petal cutter, cut out a petal that is thick at the base and thin round the edge. Soften

the edge and paint glue on the bottom half. Wrap this around a hooked 24-gauge wire. When dry, add two further tiny petals.

9 Add a small calyx and tape the stem with half-width green florists' tape.

Spray

10 Make enough flowers and buds to wire together in a spray. Steam the whole assembly lightly (see page 19).

Briar Rose Cake

This very pretty cake would be suitable for both formal
and informal occasions.

Materials

15cm (6 inch) scalloped oval
cake
23cm (9 inch) oval cake drum
Apricot glaze
500g (1lb) marzipan (almond
paste)
750g (1½ lb) cream or cham-
pagne-coloured sugarpaste
(rolled fondant)
250g (8oz) royal icing
Pink, lemon and green food
colourings
Ribbon to trim cake drum

Equipment

Icing smoothers
Flower pick
Pins (see Note)
Scriber
Paper piping bags
Nos. 0 and 2 piping tubes (tips)

Flowers

Briar Rose Spray, page 37

Preparation

1 Position the cake centrally
on the drum, and brush
with apricot glaze. Roll out the
marzipan to cover both the top
and sides of the cake in one
piece. Fit the marzipan on to the
cake, ensuring a neat, smooth
finish. Trim with a sharp knife
and polish with smoothers.
Leave to dry.

2 Roll out the sugarpaste to
coat the cake and drum at
the same time. Brush the marzipan with a little cooled, boiled
water and lift the sugarpaste
into position, smoothing well
with your hands or smoothers
and taking care to define the
shape of the cake. Push the
flower pick into the cake while
the sugarpaste is still soft.
Leave to dry.

Side design

3 Trace the side design
(pages 46–47), and hold in
position 1cm (½ inch) above the
board, using pins to hold the
paper around the inverted
curves. Push the pins into the
sugarpaste through a part of the
pattern that will be covered.
Scribe the design on to the
cake's surface, then remove the
tracing paper and pins.

4 Brush embroider the pattern, using very pale pink,
pale lemon and pale green royal
icing. When dry, pipe small bulbs
or plain shells around the base
of the cake with a no. 2 tube and
white royal icing. Finally, pipe
small dots above and below the
side pattern with a no. 0 tube
and white royal icing.

5 Trim the cake drum with
ribbon and position the
spray in the flower pick.

Note

When using pins, push them into
the cake only to the depth of the
sugarpaste; they should not go
into the marzipan or cake. Count
the pins as you put them in and
take them out, to make sure all
are removed.

Colouring Roses

Roses grow in so many shapes, sizes and colours that it would be impossible to include them all. We have chosen a small selection here to show the different colouring effects that can be achieved.

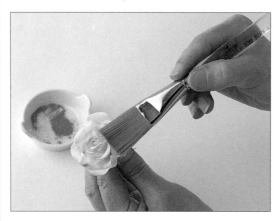

Tinged petals

Many roses have pale cream centres with lightly tinted edges. Use pale cream paste to make a rose by the five-petal cutter method (page 26), curling the petal edges back with a cocktail stick (toothpick). When the rose is completely dry, dust the edges of the petals with petal dust (blossom tint), using a large, flat brush. Steam the finished rose to seal the colour and create a light gloss (see page 19).

Above left and right: Tinged petals; below left and right: Dark centred rose

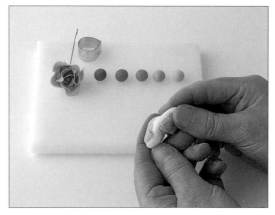

Dark-centred rose

Colour some flower paste deep pink and make the centre and first petal of the cutter rose method (page 18). Mix some more pink paste with an equal amount of white paste. Create and add two more petals. Mix the paste with an equal portion of white paste to make even paler pink paste. Create and add three more petals. Repeat the process, adding five more petals. All the petal edges are softened with a dogbone tool to create a soft, curled edge. Buds are darker than open roses, so make with darker paste only.

Below left and right: Two-colour rose

Dipped red rose

Make a white cutter rose (page 18) with six petals in total, i.e. three layers. Use a longer wire than usual. Do not make the petals too thin as they may dissolve during the dipping process. Leave to dry. Mix iso-propyl alcohol (dipping solution) with hollyberry liquid food colouring to create a very strong solution in a tall glass or jam jar. Hold the wire and dip the rose into the liquid. Lift the rose above the surface of the liquid (but still in the glass) and spin the wire between your fingers. Hang to dry in a well-ventilated room. Re-dip until the required depth of colour is achieved. NB: We recommend this method of

Above left and right: Dipped red rose

colouring for flowers that are for display purposes only – that will not come into contact with food.

Two-colour rose

In this example, we have used tangerine coloured paste and cream coloured paste and the cutter method (page 18). Roll out both pastes very thinly, lay one colour on top of the other and roll again to join them together. Cut out the petals and smooth the edges with a dog-bone tool. Attach the petals to the rose with the cream colour on the inside.

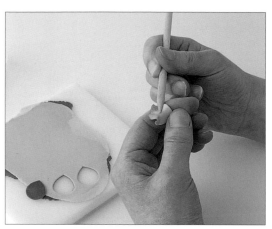

Blended colouring

In this example we have used pale yellow and burgundy paste and the cutter rose method (page 18). Roll out both pastes very thinly, lay one colour on top of the other and roll again to join them together. Cut out the petals and smooth the edges with a dogbone tool, then roll the edges with a cocktail stick (toothpick) to create lines of colour at the tips of the petals. Attach the petals to the rose with the yellow colour inside.

Lustred rose

Make a small rose using the five-petal cutter method (page 26). (We have used peach-coloured paste.) When the rose is dry, dust with copper pearl lustre colour using a large, flat brush.

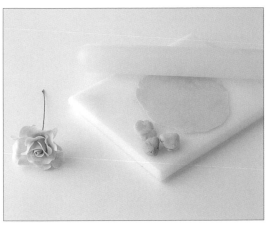

Multi-colouring

Colour three pieces of paste; the first pale pink; the second pale blueberry; the third pale grape violet. Marble all three pastes together and roll thinly. Make roses using the cutter method (page 18). To create ragged edges on some of the petals, cut the petal out and then snip with a scalpel before softening with the dogbone tool. This will produce a very fragile edge. For the very large rose illustrated above, the final outer petals were individually wired, and left to 'leather' before being added to the rest of the rose.

Fine-lined edges

This typical hybrid tea rose is made from melon-coloured paste using the cutter method (page 18). Ensure the outer petals are well curled back with a cocktail stick (toothpick). When the rose is dry, paint the edges of the petals with fine lines, using a mixture of red and brown liquid food colouring and a no. 00000 brush.

Basic Recipes

These are our favourite recipes, and they work well, but you can of course use your own versions if you prefer.

Royal Icing

60g (2oz) albumen powder
470ml (15fl oz) water
3kg (6lb) icing (confectioners')
sugar

1 Dissolve the albumen powder in the water, whisking well (the mixture will go lumpy). Cover with cling film (plastic wrap) and leave in the refrigerator to soften, preferably overnight. Remove from the refrigerator and whisk again. Strain the mixture through a fine sieve or clean tea strainer.

2 Place the albumen solution in a clean, grease-free mixer bowl, and add one third of the sugar. Beat on the lowest speed with a flat beater, not a whisk. Add half the remaining icing sugar and beat again. Finally, add the rest of the icing sugar in small portions and beat on a slow speed until the icing reaches a firm peak.

3 Clean down the sides of the bowl and cover with a damp cloth. Alternatively, place the royal icing in a lidded plastic container until required. You will need to adjust the consistency of the royal icing with water, depending upon whether you are coating or piping with it.

Modelling Marzipan

100g (3½oz) raw marzipan (such as Renmarz)
2 teaspoons liquid glucose
90g (3oz/ ½ cup) icing (confectioners') sugar

This can be made by hand. Mix the marzipan and glucose together and slowly knead in the icing sugar to give a firm paste. Store tightly wrapped in a polythene bag.

Flower Paste

1kg (2lb/6 cups) icing (confectioners') sugar
2 teaspoons gum tragacanth
4 teaspoons carboxy-methyl-cellulose (CMC)
3 teaspoons powdered gelatine
50ml (2fl oz) water
4 teaspoons white vegetable fat (shortening)
4 teaspoons liquid glucose
2 large egg whites

1 Sift the sugar, gum tragacanth and CMC together into a heatproof bowl, and place in the oven to warm.

2 Dissolve the gelatine in the water, then heat, but do not boil, until all the grains have melted and the liquid becomes clear. Add the white vegetable fat and glucose, and stir well.

3 Put the hot dry sugar and the liquid into the bowl of an electric mixer and add the egg whites. Mix on no.1 speed with a dough hook until all is well incorporated. Turn the machine speed up to full and beat until the mixture is white and 'springy'. The time taken for this will depend upon the type of machine you use. If you like a soft paste, add a little extra egg white.

4 Wrap the paste in small portions in polythene bags and place in an airtight plastic container. Place in the refrigerator to mature for 24 hours before use. You may, if you wish, freeze this paste. Microwaving the paste on 'defrost' will soften the paste if you find it too hard to soften with your hands.

Templates

Ruby Wedding Cake
(page 12)

Abcdefghijklm
nopqrstuvw
xyz

Marzipan Birthday Cake
(page 16)

Tablecloth Cake
brush embroidery pattern
(page 30)

Briar Rose Cake
(page 38)
side design

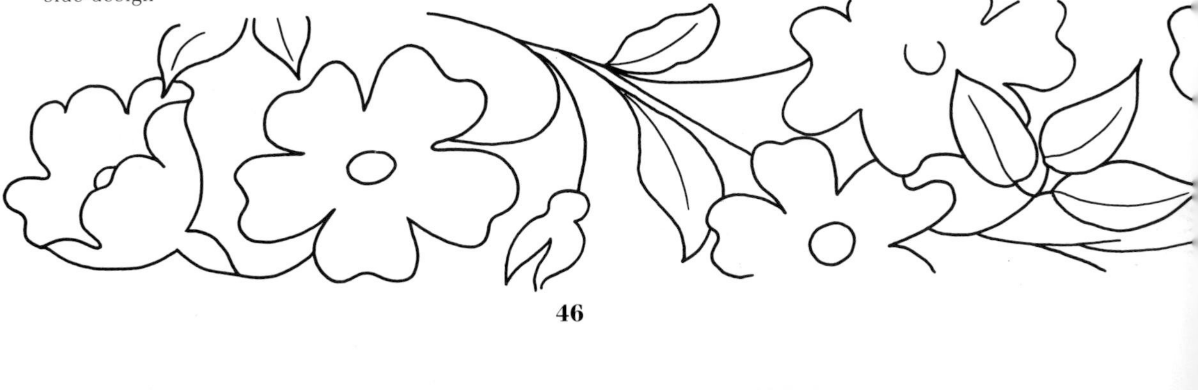

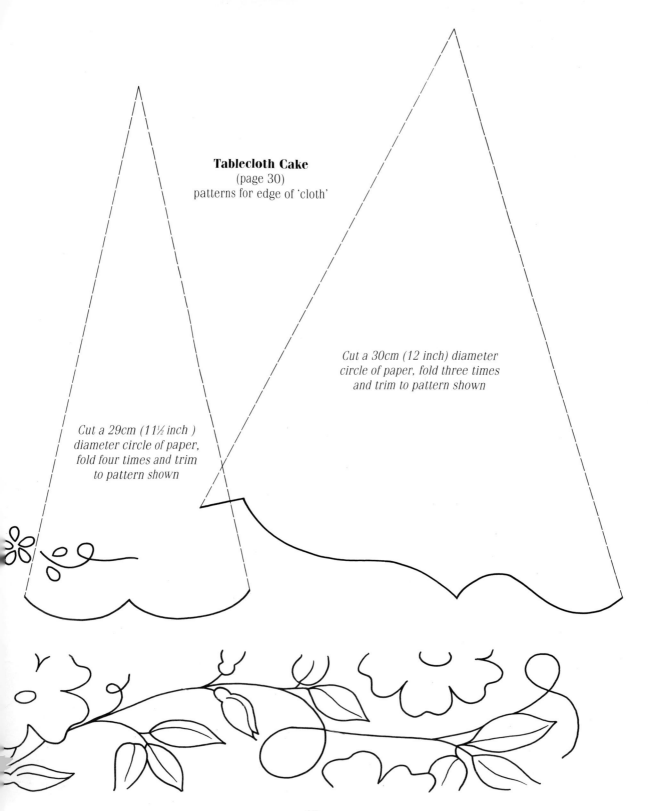

Tablecloth Cake
(page 30)
patterns for edge of 'cloth'

Cut a 30cm (12 inch) diameter
circle of paper, fold three times
and trim to pattern shown

Cut a 29cm (11½ inch)
diameter circle of paper,
fold four times and trim
to pattern shown

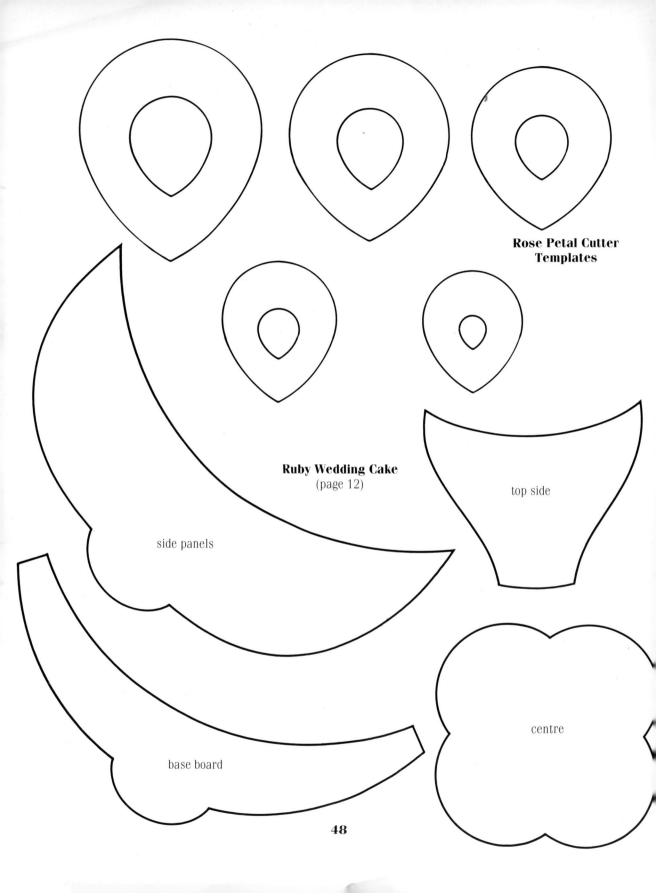

Rose Petal Cutter Templates

Ruby Wedding Cake
(page 12)

side panels

top side

base board

centre

48